Emotional Intellig

Build Rapport and Overcom.

FREYA GATES

Text Copyright © Freya Gates

All rights reserved. No part of this guide may be reproduced in any form without permission in writing from the publisher except in the case of brief quotations embodied in critical articles or reviews.

Legal & Disclaimer

The information contained in this book and its contents is not designed to replace or take the place of any form of medical or professional advice; and is not meant to replace the need for independent medical, financial, legal or other professional advice or services, as may be required. The content and information in this book has been provided for educational and entertainment purposes only.

The content and information contained in this book has been compiled from sources deemed reliable, and it is accurate to the best of the Author's knowledge, information and belief. However, the Author cannot guarantee its accuracy and validity and cannot be held liable for any errors and/or omissions. Further, changes are periodically made to this book as and when needed. Where appropriate and/or necessary, you must consult a professional (including but not limited to your doctor, attorney, financial advisor or such other professional advisor) before using any of the suggested remedies, techniques, or information in this book.

Upon using the contents and information contained in this book, you agree to hold harmless the Author from and against any damages, costs, and expenses, including any legal fees potentially resulting from the application of any of the information provided by this book. This disclaimer applies to any loss, damages or injury caused by the use and application, whether directly or indirectly, of any advice or information presented, whether for breach of contract, tort, negligence, personal injury, criminal intent, or under any other cause of action.

You agree to accept all risks of using the information presented inside this book. You agree that by continuing to read this book, where appropriate and/or necessary, you shall consult a professional (including but not limited to your doctor, attorney, or financial advisor or such other advisor as needed) before using any of the suggested remedies, techniques, or information in this book.

Table of Contents

Introduction *4*

Chapter 1 ....*5*

   The key to understanding the behaviour of children with low emotional intelligence 5
      The 4 main points to spot a child with low emotional intelligence 5
      Processes involved in the intelligence of kids 6

Chapter 2 ....*12*

   Identify the causes of "low emotional intelligence" 12
      Techniques to detect low emotional intelligence in children 13
      Consequences of low emotional intelligence in children 14
      As a parent, what to do? 14

Chapter 3 ....*16*

   5-Step system to build rapport with your children in order to improve their behaviour 16
      Step #1: Positive reinforcement, not negative 16
      Step #2: Use the "Timeout" method 16
      Step #3: Minimise unhealthy influences 17
      Step #4: Be aware of what you say to your child 18
      Step #5: Suggest an alternative 19

Chapter 4 ....*21*

   How to use the 5 steps to deal with the problems 21
      Other benefits 27

Conclusion *28*

Introduction

"In a very real sense, we have two minds, one that thinks and one that feels."
-Daniel Goleman

Family life is the first school for emotional learning: in such an intimate cauldron, we inevitably learn how to express ourselves freely and how others react to such feelings; how to think about those feelings and what choices we have when reacting; how to interpret and express hopes and fears. This emotional school works not only through what parents say or do directly to their children but also by them being role models when it comes to managing their own feelings, inclusive of those feelings that take place between husband and wife.

This ability to understand emotions is central to the theme of this book and is defined as "Emotional Intelligence". According to psychologist Peter Salovey and John Mayer of the Yale University of New Hampshire, this term serves to describe qualities such as the understanding of one's feelings, the understanding of other people's feelings and "the control of emotion in a way that intensifies life[1]".

Throughout this eBook, we will explore the origins, construct, models and components of Emotional Intelligence for children, as well as the impact on health. Linking this to the theory of the mind, we will be able to understand how we can contribute as parents to the emotional development of our beloved kids.

With a clear practical 5-step system, empowered parents can now establish rapport with our children no matter what level of emotional intelligence they possess. This book will also serve to demonstrate the applications of the system by tackling real common problems that most parents face.

---

[1] In "Emotional Intelligence: New Ability or Eclectic Traits?" John D. Mayer, Peter Salovey and David R. Caruso. American Psychologist, September 2008, Vol. 63, No. 6, pages 503 - 517.

Chapter 1

The key to understanding the behaviour of children with low emotional intelligence

Emotional intelligence is the rudder of our life because it guides every step we take, much like a guided system. This is precisely why a child with low emotional intelligence is likely to find maneuvering around society dominated by emotions as a daunting experience.

In order to facilitate help as parents, we must first learn to identify the signs of low emotional intelligence. For simplicity purposes, I will refer to a child as a 'he' throughout this book (although this is by no means exclusive to the male population!).

The 4 main points to spot a child with low emotional intelligence

1-He is unable to control his emotions

A child who is unable to control his emotions is likely to be highly irritable which can often lead to lashing out in anger.

A person who has learned to use emotional intelligence will have the innate ability to set limits when needed. He is able to express his emotional needs with assertiveness; that is by demonstrating what he needs without hurting anyone else intentionally, taking into account the feelings of those around him.

2-He has no friends

People who are emotionally intelligent usually forge strong bonds of friendship. A child with low emotional intelligence will usually find himself isolated due to the inability to recognize or respond appropriately to emotional stimuli around him. As a result, he becomes a lone wolf who has to develop himself without the benefits of the wolf pack, making the task exceedingly difficult.

3-He dislikes talking about his feelings

A sign of low emotional intelligence is that a person is clearly uncomfortable when talking about what he feels[2].

People with high emotional intelligence can express their discomfort at the precise moment in time, which is contrary to a person of low intelligence, who usually keeps a grudge bottled in. This pent-up anger can sometimes lead to a seemingly random outburst at a later point in time when his tolerance level has been surpassed, and will usually be magnified to a certain degree due to the buildup.

4-He doesn't like to be alone

Another point that helps you identify that if your kid has low emotional intelligence is the unwillingness to be alone. This clingy behaviour exhibited by the child often results in overdependence (hence missing out on the developmental milestone of independence)

What to do?

If all of the above signs aptly describe your child, then all the more you are needed as a beacon of moral support and guidance. Just remember, low emotional intelligence usually is the result of 'feeling-shame'[3] and distancing ourselves from the ones who need us most.

In order to foster a good relationship with your kid, it is necessary for you to recognize his deficiencies and be willing to help him develop his emotional intelligence. A bad start does not equate to a bad ending – the chapters below will introduce a five-step system to overcome common problems. Keep reading!

Processes involved in the intelligence of kids

Although a child may have low emotional intelligence, his mind is still similar to a sponge, ready to absorb and eager to acquire new information. In order to steepen his learning curve, we have to learn how to hone this inquisitive nature and adapt to his requirements.

---

[2] https://www.careeraddict.com/10-signs-you-lack-emotional-intelligence

[3] Megan Bruneau

For cognitive development and subsequent intelligence of the kid to mature normally, there must be a healthy biological basis, as well as a favorable and stimulating environment. This is also subject to the various eventualities or circumstances that may occur to him, such as certain diseases or trauma that may affect his biological structure. This is backed up by the renowned Swiss psychologist Jean Pieget; his theory states that cognitive development is a progressive reorganisation of mental processes as a consequence of biological maturation and environmental experience.

For Piaget, kids first assimilate a basic understanding of the world around them from their reflexes and perceptions (known as the sensory-motor stage which takes place from birth to 2 years of age).

Subsequently, a more abstract level of thinking begins to develop in the kid, in which a more complex intelligence emerges. The assimilation mechanisms and the accommodation to the environment cause the child to gradually incorporate, conceptualise and internalize his experiences.

How to measure the emotional intelligence of kids

The benefits of proper emotional management in kids are not only limited to social relationships and self-esteem. There are numerous scientific studies that have shown that its advantages extend to many other areas of life, such as:

- ✓ Greater satisfaction and success both personally and professionally[4]
- ✓ Less dependence on addictions[5]
- ✓ Better immune system and health in general[6]
- ✓ Reduction of anxiety and stress[7]
- ✓ Greater satisfaction with marriage[8]
- ✓ Greater charisma in his social and professional circle[9]

Activity Sheet: Test to evaluate the Emotional Intelligence of a kid[10]

First part

In each sentence you must assess, on a scale of 1 to 7, the capacity described (1-3 being low grade capacity, 4-7 being high grade capacity). Before answering, try to think of real situations in which your child has had to use that capacity.

---

[4] O'Boyle Jr., 2010

[5] Zysberg, 2013 y UAB, 2007

[6] Martins et al., 2010

[7] Lusch & Serpkeuci, 1990

[8] Eslami, 2014

[9] [9] Walter V. Clarke Associates, 1997

[10] Test taken from Weisinger, H. (2001). Emotional intelligence at work. Madrid: Javier Vergara. (P. 334-341). Adaptation of Mireya Vivas, Second and Third Part.

1. Identify the changes of the physiological stimulus	
2. Relax in a situation of pressure	
3. Acting productively when he is angry	
4. Acting productively in situations of anxiety	
5. Reassure himself fast when he is angry	
6. Associate different physical signs with different emotions	
7. Use the inner dialogue to control emotional states	
8. Communicate feelings effectively	
9. Think about negative feelings without being upset	
10. Keep calm when he is the target of others' anger	
11. Know when he has negative thoughts	
12. Know when his "inner discourse" is positive.	
13. Know when he starts to get angry	
14. Know how he interprets events	
15. Know what feelings he currently uses	
16. Communicate precisely what he experiences	
17. Identify the information that influences his interpretations	
18. Identify his mood changes	
19. Know when he is on the defensive	
20. Calculate the impact that his behaviour has on others	
21. Know when he does not communicate with meaning	
22. Get moving when he needs it	

23. Recover quickly after a setback	
24. Complete long-term assignments within the expected time	
25. Show understanding towards others	
26. Engage intimate conversations with others	
27. Mediate in the conflicts of others	
28. Influence others directly or indirectly	
29. Build trust in others	
30. Develop consensus with others	
31. Make others feel good	
32. Use effective interpersonal communication techniques	

Second part

Add the assigned values from the above table in the appropriate category:

Self-Awareness

1.___ 6.___ 11.___ 12.___ 13.___ 14.___ 15.___ 17.___ 18.___ 19.___ 20.___ 21.___

Control of Emotions

1.___ 2.___ 3.___ 4.___ 5.___ 7.___ 9.___ 10.___ 13.___ 27.___

Self-Motivation

7.___ 22.___ 23.___ 25.___ 26.___ 27.___ 28.___

Connect Well

8.___ 10.___ 16.___ 19.___ 20.___ 29.___ 30.___ 31.___ 32.___

Emotional Counselling

8.___ 10.___ 16.___ 18.___

Reflections based on the results:

_____
_____
_____
_____

Third Part

Study the results and identify the skills your child should improve on, taking what was done in the second part as a reference. Identify two of the emotional intelligence capacities that you and your child should focus on most:

1. _____

2. _____

Finally, determine some specific tasks that will help him master these two emotional intelligence capabilities:

_____
_____
_____

Chapter 2

Identify the causes of "low emotional intelligence"

"Our emotions can be our greatest strength or our worst weakness. All depends on how we handle them." Anonymous

Low emotional intelligence is a result of various factors; usually it can be due to a chemical imbalance in the brain, such as decreased serotonin (in cases of depression), or variation in the level of dopamine and serotonin in cases such as bipolar disorder. Additionally, things like stress, abuse, low self-esteem, pain, abandonment or loss can also produce low emotional intelligence.

1- The stress of daily life

As adults, we can attest to the fact that daily life can indeed be stressful, and this is no different to your kid. Being put in unfamiliar scenarios can stress a child as he is out of his comfort zone, especially if he has low emotional intelligence. This is the main reasons why he can appear to be clingy when he is about to be separated from you.

2- The breakup of a relationship

If a relationship goes sour, you might find yourself going through the vicious process of anger, resentment, nostalgia and unhappiness. These are complicated emotions that could affect children in a profound way and may take time to overcome. However, there is no need to despair because there is always another flip side of the coin.

"Difficulties prepare ordinary people for extraordinary destinations." C.S. Lewis.

Numerous discoveries suggest that the emotional adjustment in life is deeply influenced by the quality that exists in the relationship between the mother and the family[11]. Being close to the family during these difficult times will aid the child's transition to new changes in his daily routine.

---

[11] Rodríguez, 2000.

Techniques to detect low emotional intelligence in children

"The demands that the world presents to us are so different that, in order to face them, we need to manage different bits of intelligence." (Siegfried and Gabriele, 1997).

Baena (2003) mentions 4 different techniques to detect low emotional intelligence of children.

Technique #1: The game

A child's playtime is very important for his cognitive development. Through play, he learns to discover and experiment, to measure qualities of objects, tests his reflexes to stimulants, observes cause-effect relationships, situates himself in space and calculates distances. This is why the common misconception of play as being unnecessary and not being beneficial is misguided as this is actually an important stage for the child's learning curve.

Technique #2: Smile

Serotonin is very important for the emotional life of children as it influences many body systems such as body temperature, blood pressure, digestion and sleep. In fact, it can even help to cope with all kinds of stress by inhibiting an overload of energy in the brain. Elevated levels of serotonin are associated with decreased aggression and impulsivity.

Technique #3: Issues related to the existence

A child of high emotional intelligence questions everything with regard to existence. This inquisitive nature is a good sign that you child is developing normally (although the constant barrage of questions can indeed be tedious at times!)

Technique #4: Vocabulary

The vocabulary of a child with low emotional intelligence may be limited due to the poor assimilation of information. This also ties in to point 3 – naturally non-inquisitive behavior leads to a narrower range of vocabulary.

Consequences of low emotional intelligence in children

So what are the consequences of low emotional intelligence?

1 - They say and do things impulsively, not realising that what they say and do have consequences and may affect others. This makes socialisation difficult for them and often makes them alienated.

2 - They are easily frustrated and this often leads to them being "bad losers". This often gets in the way of the child's development because he will find difficult tasks daunting and hence willingly turns to anger rather than productivity (hence not finishing what he starts).

3 – Emotions are often bottled up due to difficulty in expressing them out (pent-up), which causes emotional and physical damage to the body in the long run.

4 – Children miss out on the joy that life brings because of their resentment towards the world (linked to point 3)

5 – They find it difficult to adapt to changes (transitions to different stages of their life) and this can lead them to missing out on developmental milestones.

As a parent, what to do?

If you are a parent or you work with kids, you have a great responsibility to help him socialise and improve his emotional intelligence. The examples you set for them through your attitude and reactions will be their guide and mirror.

Children often process experiences at their most simplistic level, thus using logic and reasoning will take time. Here are some tips to help you resonate with them:

***Tip #1**: Name his emotions*

Anger, nervousness, envy …, have you ever wondered if your kid can understand and differentiate between them? Although it may seem obvious to you, he may not know the reason for feeling in a certain way even though he feels the emotion. Begin to verbalise and classify his feelings in order to help him to understand them. "I understand that you are nervous because it is the first time you are here…"

Tip #2: *Try to talk about his feelings*

Be interested in how he is feeling and explore the emotion, including how it came about. Teach him to express it with moderation and self-control, and perhaps share what you do when you feel the same way as him.

Tip #3: *Give him options*

If he has reacted to a situation inappropriately, explain to him what he should have done instead of purely reprimanding him. Let him know the importance of apologising if he has done something that has hurt or agitated someone else.

Tip #4: *Encourage his empathy*

Let your child know what other people might be feeling by asking him to put himself in the shoes of someone else. If his best friend is crying, first ask him what he thinks he should do. If he is unsure, explain that it is as simple as imagining what he would need if he were in his place e.g. a warm hug.

Tip #5: *Become his example*

Would you like to be yelled at if you didn't know how to do something right? Similarly, if your kid does not act in a precise manner, do not yell at him. Just remember - you are his greatest reference in life. Keep that in mind because just as they copy the "bad", they will reproduce the "good".

Chapter 3

5-Step system to build rapport with your children in order to improve their behaviour

In order to improve your child's behaviour, you must first build rapport with him. In this chapter, we will learn 5 steps to do this which will be applicable to some common problems that are highlighted later.

Step #1: Positive reinforcement, not negative

Reward the good behaviour:

You can use innumerable variants for positive reinforcement. A compliment or a smile can be excellent positive reinforcers, as well as a reward system. This can come in the form of various activities (going to the park, playing in the yard, visiting the zoo, watching a movie, etc.) or material incentives (a toy, for example).

It is important to show gratitude to your kid and show him that you are proud of his accomplishments. In this way, the likelihood of repeated good behavior will increase, and a stronger foundation of self-esteem will be built.

Ignore the bad behaviour:

It is important to clarify that children need and want attention from adults. Therefore, any attention given will always be a plus point, even if comes in the form of a punishment or reprimand. Just remember, attention is a positive reinforcement and should only be given to a desirable behaviour.

Positive reinforcement has very good results if applied correctly and judiciously. With patience and affection, we can work towards achieving a desirable outcome in the behaviour of our children.

Step #2: Use the "Timeout" method

You must determine in advance what behaviour will result in a timeout e.g. tantrums or aggressive behaviour. Once this is done, choose a neutral place for the child to be associated with the "timeout" that could be uninteresting like a chair, corner or playpen. If you are outside, consider using a vehicle or a nearby area where he can sit during the "timeout".

When unacceptable behaviour surfaces, tell the child that he must behave himself or he will receive a "timeout". If your kid continues to misbehave, take him calmly to the designated area.

If possible, keep track of how long your kid has been in the "timeout". Use a stopwatch so that the kid is aware of when this ends. The duration should usually be short (usually 1 minute for each year of age) and should start immediately when the child has reached the destination. Stay close so that the kid sees you or can hear you, but do not talk to him. If the kid attempts to leave the designated area, return him calmly and restart the timer.

Step #3: Minimise unhealthy influences

While the kid is young, you will be responsible for what he watches on television. While factoring in this decision, you should take into account:

- ✓ Each program is made for different age groups. A 5-year-old child is likely to be bored easily if he is watching a show made for a 2-year-old.

- ✓ Accompany your child when he watches television. This way, you can supervise his viewing habits as well as monitor the time he spends on this activity. (You can integrate this into a reward system as mentioned in Step #1 e.g. If you finish your homework, you can watch an hour of cartoons) No matter how well he behaves, bear in mind he should not be spending too much time watching the television as this can lead to myopia at a young age.

- ✓ Choose programs that have educational content, deliver values and teach them to be creative. A good example of this is Sesame Street.

- ✓ Cartoons are a good way to deliver complex messages – do not overlook these as this could be a good way for the child to learn how to interact with his community.

It is imperative that you provide him with alternative activities that are entertaining and edifying at the same time. Make sure his daily activity is balanced and try to bring in sports whenever possible – this encourages valuable time outside where he can socialise with other people and keep himself fit and healthy.

Step #4: Be aware of what you say to your child

Children often believe that "good manners", "sharing" and "taking turns" apply exclusively to them. So, when adults share, let your child know.

e.g. "Daddy is sharing his drink with Mummy. How kind and generous you are!"

Some common phrases that should be avoided

1. "Learn from your brother"

Comparisons are never a good thing because all they create are inadequacy and jealousy, both of which aren't entirely healthy. This also creates a low self-esteem within the child which is very damaging.

2. "Aren't you ashamed to behave like that?"

This fosters shame and is not constructive – a more productive way would be to ask him for the reason behind his behaviour and how he thinks it makes other people feel.

3. "If you don't do this, I will punish you"

Threatening is using fear to achieve your goal and when a parent does it to a child, could lead to eroding the trust that he has placed in his parent. You would also be effectively teaching him that intimidation is a viable option in order to get what he wants.

4. "I have had enough"

This can be misinterpreted as despair and ultimately giving up on the kid which is exactly the vibe you do not want to give. As parents, we need to constantly encourage our children, no matter how hard the obstacle may be. They will eventually learn never to give up in the face of adversity, just like how their parents persevered.

5. "Just do it without any question"

This discourages the child to be inquisitive which inhibits his learning curve as we have mentioned in the earlier chapter. We should always tell the child the reasons behind our decisions so that it can help them be empathetic, that is to understand and subsequently learn to put themselves into other people's shoes.

Step #5: Suggest an alternative

Whenever you apply a limit to a kid's behavior, try to indicate an acceptable alternative. It will sound less negative and your kid will feel compensated e.g. "that's my lipstick and it's not for playing; have some brushes to paint instead." By offering alternatives, you are teaching him that his feelings and wishes are acceptable, acknowledging them in the process.

Being Tactful

By wording it diplomatically, you can give the child a choice whilst simultaneously achieving the desired outcome. Examples of this would be:

"It's bath time; would you prefer the shower or tub?"

"It's time to get dressed, do you choose your clothes, or do I?"

Some tips in the process of solving problems

Tip #1: Don't be offended by your kid's NO

Do not confuse the "NO" with a lack of respect. Your kid is just "asking" if he really has to.

Tip #2: Don't punish your kid for saying "NO"

A better way of getting him to be more cooperative is to show him what he misses out on when he says "NO". If he pushes his plate of broccoli away, take it and eat some, showing him how tasty it is in the process. An alternative would be to offer a bonus if he does not say "NO" e.g. some tasty chocolate for finishing his greens (positive reinforcement).

Tip #3: Don't demand drastic changes in activity

Before asking your kid who is playing in the yard with his friends to come home, tell him he still has five minutes left to play. Give him something to look forward to when he does leave e.g. "Time to eat your favourite dino nuggets!"

By helping your child to manage his emotions well and increase his emotional intelligence, you will simultaneously learn a lot from your own. In the next chapter, we will learn how to apply these 5 steps to common problems associated with low emotional intelligence. Keep reading!

Chapter 4

How to use the 5 steps to deal with the problems

The teaching of positive behavior begins with the establishment of coherent limits and norms that are reinforced in a consistent manner. Appropriate behavior is also encouraged when you, as a parent, establish routines and schedules e.g. taking a bath, eating, taking a nap, sleeping, and doing activities inside and outside your home.

Teaching self-control helps your kid learn to control his actions. This starts with learning to make good decisions. Often, children get upset when their needs or wants are not met immediately. If your kid has that feeling while you are working to help him develop emotional intelligence, you can teach him strategies to deal with this frustration.

A good start is to guide your kid to use words that express his frustration, such as teaching him to say: "I am angry! I want to have _____ ". You can then guide the behavior by offering good alternatives e.g. "Instead of having ice-cream, how about playing a game of I Spy (I spy with my little eye something that begins with....)?"

Below are some common problems associated with children who have low emotional intelligence. With the 5 steps listed above, we can now tackle these with new assured confidence.

Problem # 1: kids are not noticing how their negative behavior is affecting others

<u>*The solution*</u> *(Step #4: Be Aware of What You Say to Your Child)*

- ***Start at home***

When looking for the factors that influence your child's behavior, first consider what happens in the home. Children who are exposed to shouting, insults, disparagement, harsh criticism, or physical anger from a sibling, parent, or caregiver can mimic that behaviour in other environments under the assumption that those behaviours are normal.

- ***Teach children to be respectful and kind***

Respect is an attitude. Being respectful helps your kid succeed in life. If your kid does not respect his peers, authority figures, or even himself, it is almost impossible for him to succeed.

A respectful kid is careful with his belongings and responsibilities and gets along well with his peers.

Schools teach children the value of respect, but it is parents who have the greatest influence on children when it comes to learning to be respectful.

In fact, until kids show respect in their home, they do not usually show respect outside such as a school or park.

- *Be aware of your child's social life*

Show an interest in the child's social life by frequently asking them whether they have had a good day or what they have been up to. This way, it will be easier to correct any possible anti-social behaviour, by paying attention to his descriptive tone even if he does not tell the full story (read between the lines).

Problem # 2: Your child is not noticing when people are upset or sending off signals that they are angry

The solution (Step #1: Positive Reinforcement, Not Negative)

- *Observe and take notes*

Keeping track of when your child is being impulsive will give you valuable information. Your notes can help you and the professionals who are working with your child work backwards to find out the details of what is happening.

- *Reward him when your child is being good*

Praise your child when he is able to handle his impulses. Teach him what signs to look out for when people are upset and how his actions reap consequences. Through positive reinforcement, the child will learn to associate the correct response with a positive feeling, in this case the feeling of being praised. Subconsciously, this will also lead to the child learning the importance of limits and boundaries, so as to not overstep them.

Problem # 3: Hidden anxiety and does not trust others

<u>*The solution*</u> *(Step #4: Be Aware of What You Say to Your Child)*

- *Prepare him for new situations*

Preparing your kid for new situations by helping him to label and contextualise his feelings so that he is familiar with them. Familiarity is the ultimate counter to anxiety.

- *Change the rhythm of life*

If your rhythm of life seems hasty, you may wish to adopt a slower rhythm to allow the kid to explore his outer and inner world at his own pace. Allow him to connect with his environment and the people around him without any hassle or limitations.

- *Constant Encouragement*

Constant encouragement and emotional support will help your child get over his anxiety and trust issues. Acknowledge his fear and quantify it – let your child know that if he listens to your advice, the unpleasant feeling will go away gradually with time. Establishing trust with him will allow him to trust others as well as the experiences are aligned.

Problem #4: Really possessive/obsessive (over a friend)

"Possessiveness is nothing more than a clear sign of unsafe personality which is full of fears." Daniel Georg Guttfreund

<u>*The solution*</u> *(Step #4: Be Aware of What You Say to Your Child)*

- *Work to have a good self-esteem*

The first thing that must be done to heal a controlling personality is to notice that there is a problem. The root of having a possessive nature is insecurity. In order to combat this, you will need to work on your child's self-esteem.

Self-esteem can be fostered by doing things that give satisfaction when goals are achieved. These are some important things to do with your child:

✓ Recognize his qualities

- Help him improve what he doesn't do so well.

- When he is wrong about something, it's good to know what he is wrong about, but it's even better if he knows what he should do instead, so explain to him how it's done!

- Accept him with his qualities and his defects ... if you don't accept him he will not be accepted either. It is impossible to be perfect and you must show him that it is impossible; otherwise, he will be unhappy looking for perfection.

- Do not force him to be what he is not ... he needs to be himself, to find his own identity. He has not come to this world to fulfill your expectations, but to construct his life.

- Express your love, either verbally or through non-verbal language (looks, caresses, hugs, etc.). If he perceives your love he will also learn to love himself and love others.

- Trust your kid; this will make him learn to trust himself.

- *Help him control his anxiety*

Another reason why your kid can be controlling is that he is full of anxiety, always thinking about the worst that can happen in a situation or be being terrified of facing the unknown. Similar to problem #3, help him get used to unfamiliar situations while being patient.

- *Propose new challenges*

As a parent, you can build your kid's confidence by offering attractive feats such as learning to ride a bike or responsibilities such as feeding your fish. This type of activity requires effort and implies trust.

Problem # 5: screaming very often and being upset

<u>*The solution*</u> *(Step #3: Minimise Unhealthy Influences, Step #2: Use the "Timeout" Method)*

- *Speak when the crisis has passed*

One of the things you should not do is try to reason with a kid who is furious. You want to encourage the practice of the art of negotiation when you are both calm.

- *Remain calm and be consistent*

You are in a better position to teach when you are in control of your own emotions. Responding with anger or criticism tends to escalate the kid's aggression, whether verbal or physical. By remaining calm, you will be setting a good example and teaching him the type of behavior you wish to see.

- *Use the "Timeout" Method*

Your kid needs to know what the consequences of his negative behaviour are, in this instance isolation time.

- *Prepare a toolbox to calm him*

Both you and your child need to build what experts call a toolbox to calm down e.g. breathing slowly. There are many techniques out there but "the good thing about breathing is that it is always available".

Benefits in increasing the Emotional Intelligence of kids

The benefits of increased intelligence in children are immense. You, as a parent, are the basis on which your kid will build his emotional well-being thanks to physiological, cognitive and emotional tools. This includes knowing how to control emotions, quantify and manage them.

There are studies that indicate that positive emotions improve the immune system and help prevent diseases because they result in a decrease in pain, reduction of blood pressure and a decrease in levels of adrenaline associated with anxiety. Conversely, poor emotional management can undermine health by reducing the defenses of the immune system.

Above all, there will be a mutual empathy between you and your child. Understanding your child can only lead to a closer relationship and allows you to provide the extra layers of emotional support where they are needed.

Other benefits

The increasing of Emotional Intelligence tends to:

- ✓ Improve communication in the family environment
- ✓ Strengthen affective bond
- ✓ Strengthen knowledge between parents and children
- ✓ Increase confidence and security in children.
- ✓ Increase the happiness of the family

Remember, love is the most powerful energy that exists to create, build, act and grow. This will sustain a person with greater or lesser strength to face the challenges of life.

Conclusion

Throughout this eBook, we have learnt several important points. We have understood that the concept of low emotional intelligence is the lack of ability to control and understand emotions, which create different feelings such as anxiety, anger and sadness, among others. Improving emotional intelligence is directly linked to improving social relations.

Emotional intelligence is known to contribute to 80% of success (personal, social, work and business), while factors and cognitive skills make up the remaining 20%. So, it is prudent to work the emotional factor with greater emphasis in order to achieve success.

Children, from an early age, do not know how to express signs of empathy with others. Quite often, they do not understand their own feelings and emotions, so it is essential that parents and the educational school work hand in hand to help them overcome this and develop normally.

You also have to take into account the importance of teaching your kid to channel the accumulation of negative emotions that will be faced during his life. This way, the child will be happier and the doors will be open to a less violent and more prepared society on a personal scale.

Finally, by helping to increase your child's Emotional Intelligence, you have indirectly increased your own. The door to emotional literacy is always open and, just as it is the schools' job to educate, parents have to take the initiative to make sure their child does not miss out on developmental milestones. Companies and professionals who want to achieve success in the environment of specialisation and diversity that characterises the modern world must have awareness of their emotions and how to intelligently harness them.

-- Freya Gates

Made in the USA
Lexington, KY
29 March 2019